Table of Contents

Bonding with your serval

The most important thing to do is to teach your Serval to trust you. Trust comes before bonding. There are many ways to teach your serval to trust you. You can use special treats, food, toys, play, and nap times as tools to help you with this. Always be patient, and do not react to bad behavior with threatening reactions. If you have to reprimand your kitten for doing something wrong, just use a low firm voice and body language to get the message across. You can use time out by putting him into his kennel for a couple of hours. It is always best to try not to punish bad behavior but to encourage good behavior. By this I mean, if you notice your kitten going to the litter box or using the scratch post or anything else you have been trying to encourage him to do. Stop what you're doing right away and recognize him by giving him treats and telling him what a good boy he is and spend a little while playing with him. It is important to let him get used to how your voice sounds when you are pleased and when you are displeased. Your serval will want to please you and will shy away from you when you are angry.

Servals do better when they are in a calm environment. They are easily spooked when someone moves to quickly or when they hear a loud unexpected noise. This is one reason I do not recommend a serval pet for parents with younger children. Wait until your children are old enough to learn to be calm and predictable.

Servals do get along with other animals especially when they grow up together. Just be careful when introducing small animals to adult servals. They could see them as prey if they are smaller than the size of a full grown rabbit.

When your serval is young teach them to play with toys and no other body parts. It seems harmless when they are tiny little precious kittens but when they become bigger they will continue the same behavior and they could easily hurt you with their adult teeth and claws. Start handling his paws and messaging them whenever you have the chance. Once he learns to relax you can start clipping his nails. The best time to do this is when they are napping. You will need to clip them at least once a week. At first you may only get one or two nails at a time. But before long, if you are consistent and you don't hurt your baby by clipping to deep, he will learn to enjoy his message time with you.

Do not feed directly from your hands because your serval may start to associate food with hands and he could accidentally bite you when you are reaching out to pet him. A chicken leg looks a lot like the thumb and the meaty part of the hand. Instead, try feeding them by placing a little bit of their favorite food on a plate near you and stroke them while they eat. This will teach trust.

If your serval seems overly aggressive while eating you should try feeding them more frequently. A serval should be fed at least twice a day. They become aggressive with their food when they are not being fed often enough.

Another way to bond with your Serval is to lie down on the floor with their favorite toy in hand. Standing can make them feel uneasy, so meet them eye to eye. Use a stick toy or a ball to throw.

Servals are very playful, as you will soon find out. They will bring you things to throw. They are natural retrievers and they love playing fetch, tug of war and catch. You will need to play with your baby for at least 30 minutes twice a day.

Some servals love water and don't be surprised if your pet serval joins you while you are taking a shower or bath. They will enjoy having a kiddie pool filled with balls and other toys in their outdoor enclosure.

Serval Housing

The African Serval is a good sized, active cat. They need to have plenty of space to run around and play. Your Serval will need a large enclosure outside. It is recommended that the outside enclosure be attached to your house with a pet door for the serval to enter and leave as he wishes. This is important because constant interaction with your serval is what keeps him social. The pet door will allow him to go outside for exercise or just lie in the sun and play in the grass. Servals need direct sun in order to break down calcium and other nutrients in their body. If your serval does not get enough direct unfiltered sunlight they may develop a bone density disease.
Serval's enjoy the rain and will lay in it as long as the weather is warm.

The outdoor enclosure should be at least 8 feet tall and 20 ft. by 20 ft. The top should be covered in order to prevent your Serval from jumping out. Build a jungle gym inside with lots of perches, balls and large hard plastic toys. Water features are always a good bonus. You can put minnows in the water for a little fun. Supply a fully enclosed area for them to get in out of the elements.

Animals kept in clean and sanitary environments are exposed to fewer diseases than those kept in dirty environments so make sure you clean their environment regularly. Pathogenic virus/bacteria/fungus can grow in filth and this kind of environment often damages the serval's immunity. The buildup of ammonia in poorly cleaned, inadequately ventilated enclosures damages the lungs making servals more susceptible to respiratory diseases.

The floors should be non-porous because you don't want any scents to be absorbed into the surface. The room should be mopped and wiped down regularly. Before you clean you will need to send all the cats out. Block the entrance to keep them out. Scrub and mop the floors daily with VPB mixture (10 percent white vinegar, 10 percent baking soda, 10 percent peroxide, 70 percent water). This solution is excellent for removing urine scents and does not have a strong odor. You will need to also scrub and mop the floors once a week with a 10 percent solution of bleach. After it dry's mop over it with the VPB mixture to remove any of the bleach residue.

You must keep their litter boxes scooped every day because servals do not naturally cover up their poo like domestic cats do. Clean the litter boxes once a week with a bleach solution. It is a good idea to keep your litter boxes in the outside enclosed area in order to train your serval to only go to the bathroom in the outside area and not in your house. This will help detour any future spraying habits.

Puma and her baby

Litter Box Training

When you receive your kitten from a breeder, you must teach your kitten where the litter boxes are. Place the kitten in a small room with a litter box in every corner. In the wild servals use one or two spots in their territory and tend to stick with those spots. You can try puppy pads or pine pellets if your kitten does not like the litter or tries to eat it. Leave the kitten in the room for a few weeks and then you can slowly increase his boundaries. Don't ever yell at your kitten. If they make a mistake just pick them up and take them to their litter box. If you see the kitten continue going to different spots put a litter box in those spots. You may need to show your kitten the litter box several times, but once they recognize this as their spot, they will learn to return on their own. When you discover any accidents, you must clean the spot thoroughly. NO AMMONIA cleaning products, this will only encourage your Serval to use this place again. Only use enzyme-based odor removers. The VPB mixture works great!

You may have to start over from the beginning several times before your kitten learns where the litter boxes are. Start again by putting them back in the same room for a few more days and continue the same steps as before.

Keep in mind that sudden refusal to use the litter box may mean that your cat may have a UTI or some other type of infection. Check for an abnormally strong smelling odor in the urine and if the odor is unusually foul, have your kitten examined by a vet ASAP.

Serval Vet Care

If you decide to vaccinate, killed vaccines are recommended. Servals can become ill if you use live or modified vaccines. You should wait until they are at least 9 weeks old before vaccinating because servals mature slower than domestic cats and they are still developing their natural antibodies for the first several months of their life. You don't want to disrupt this process by introducing vaccines.

You also have to be careful not to use vaccines that contain a lot of toxins, because servals have smaller livers than domestic cats and it takes a lot longer for servals to rid the toxins from their blood stream. Killed vaccines offer very little protection from a virus but they are the safest. Talk to you exotic vet about what vaccines they recommend. The key here is not to over vaccinate and only give what is needed. Keep in mind if you do decide to use modified live virus vaccines try to find a brand that has the least amount of toxins. It is a wise idea to give your serval an IV of fluids to help flush the toxins from her blood stream after every shot. I recommend vaccinating if your serval has any possibility of coming into contact with any non-vaccinated animal.

If you are required to get rabies vaccine use the one made by Maerial without preservatives for cats only. The practice of vaccinating our animals to prevent disease is a subject of a great deal of debate. Heated discussions arise over what to vaccinate with, when to vaccinate, who to vaccinate, and even whether to vaccinate at all. Every side has strong arguments for why their way is the right way and can show statistics and tell horror stories to prove their point. The bottom line is that there is no such thing as a risk free life. Each one of us must make our own decisions, and no matter what decision we make, there will be risks involved

Serval Harness Training

Start harness training your serval as soon as you get them settled in. They must be harness trained if you want to take them with you on errands and joy rides. You should start training them at a young age. Don't use a regular collar because servals can wiggle out of them in a hurry if they become spooked. Get the dog type harness that fits snug and is made from sturdy materials. Also purchase a gps collar from

www.com-spec.com/thecatlocator/about_locator.htm . The one clip, easy to fasten kind of harness works the best because they can be put on quickly. Your serval will not sit still for very long while you put the harness on, so be quick.

You should start harness training your serval by letting them wear the harness around the house without a leash. Keep an eye on them and be sure they don't get hung on something and choke themselves.

After your kitten has worn the harness for a couple of weeks introduce a leash with no tension. Practice taking them on walks in the house. Play fetch in order to get them moving. This will help them get used to the feel of the tension. Your serval will not cooperate at first but with practice they will learn to enjoy walks and joy rides. Be sure there are no large dogs or strange new things lurking around when you take your serval out for walks. Servals are easily spooked and a scared serval is stronger than you would imagine. If he escapes he will be hard to catch.

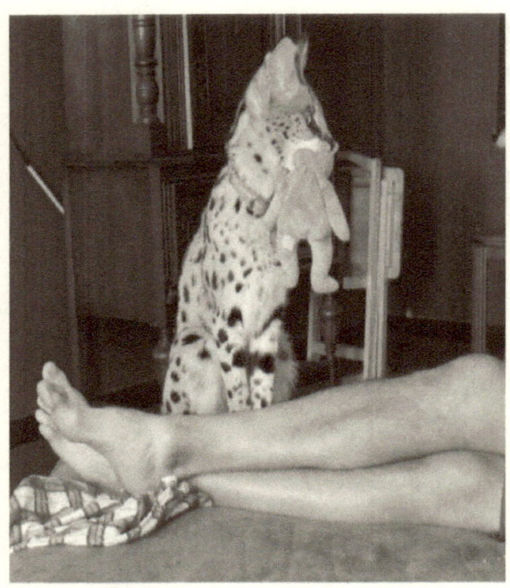

Serval Safety Issues

Servals are usually very healthy animals if kept on the right diet and in a clean environment but it's important to be prepared in case your serval gets sick. Your Serval can't tell you what is bothering them so you have to be the one to look for signs of illness. Always keep an eye on your serval and look for any signs of illness, which include drastic mood changes, vomiting, diarrhea, straining while urinating, lethargy and loss of appetite for more than a day. Particularly, you should be wary of diarrhea. In young servals, this can dehydrate them in a few hours and they may need fluids intravenously. If you see diarrhea more than two days in a row, it would be a good idea to have a vet check them out. Diarrhea can sometimes result from a change in diet or stress from traveling. But this usually goes away within 24 hours.

If there is any reason that you suspect that your Serval is ill, the best thing is to take your serval to an exotic pet veterinarian. Have a vet already picked out before you receive your pet serval. Call the exotic veterinarian of your choice and let them know that you will be using them if you run into any trouble. It is a good Idea to try and take your serval on regular visits to the vet in order for the vet and serval to get acquainted

Fleas are a big problem in the summer months and it is always a challenge when applying flea spray. I try to stay away from as many poisons as I can and stick with more holistic products. Diatomaceous earth is used to get rid of worms, parasites and fleas. You can safely use it in their food, bedding and on their fur. Diatomaceous earth is made up of tiny microscopic Diatomaceous earth, also known as D.E., or diatomite, is a naturally occurring, soft, siliceous sedimentary rock that is easily crumbled into a fine white to off-white powder. The fine powder absorbs fats from the outer layer of the flea and causes it to dehydrate.

When servals are young, toys that are made for domestic cats will be fine. But when your serval becomes a little bigger they will easily destroy them. Keep an eye on the toys, and when you notice the toys are being destroyed quickly, it's time to graduate to the hard plastic dog toys. If the toys are too soft or small there is a big possibility your serval will swallow them and cause a blockage in their throat or intestines. This is usually fatal! Serval kittens like to chew like a puppy. It is a good idea to have plenty of toys that they can chew on. Pick hard plastic toys not soft plastic. The soft plastic is easily chewed and consumed. Also monitor the toys constantly and replace them when needed. They will collect small stuffed animals and its ok but as soon as the stuffing starts to come out of them either throw the stuffed animal away or sew it up. You don't what your serval swallowing this stuff, because it can cause blockages. Also plastic bags and Styrofoam needs to be put away or thrown away. Learn to monitor your house and their enclosures for potentially dangerous items and warn others in your family to do the same.

If you provide your servals with plenty of toys, they will be less likely to chew on other things. If they begin chewing on electrical cords, a good solution is to spray the exposed cords with bitter apple spray (available at pet stores). You can also run your cords through a pvc pipe to provide a protective cover. Servals chew when they are young because they are cutting teeth. As they mature their chewing habits decrease.

I personally do not recommend declawing. Start messaging your kittens paws at a young age and they will grow accustom to having their paws handled. Keep this up whenever you get a chance. Wait until they are asleep and start to clip their nails using regular human toe nail clippers. You only want to clip the tips off. Have your vet or someone else experienced at this show you how to do this. You don't want to injure your baby and cause them to become scared when you try to clip their nails. As they get older you will have to move to a different type clipper made for large cat claws and you can use a nail cover called soft claws. I order the small to medium sized dog sized from Amazon. They are very inexpensive and easy to apply.

Be sure all children are supervised while they are around the Serval. Teach your child to be calm and gentle around your serval. If your serval is mistreated by children, they may develop a fear of children that will stick with them permanently.

Servals usually like other animals and will welcome play with almost any animal after they have had time to get acquainted with each other. Once the

Serval is close to full-grown however, you should exercise caution when introducing a new small pet, such as a young kitten or puppy. They may think that they are a chew toy or prey and hurt them.

Serval kitten Diet

When you first receive your serval kitten they are usually around 9 weeks old. They have their first shots at 9 weeks old and your kitten may be still drinking a bottle. If they are I recommend Fox Valley formula for kittens. To prepare the formula you should warm the water to at least 100 degrees before adding it to the powder to insure a good smooth mix with no clumps. Purchase a container that has a no leak sealed top that you can use for mixing and storing your formula. I also recommend a whisk ball like the kind you find in protein shake containers. This is used to mix the powder and separate any clumps. I use the PetAg bottles which can be ordered from Amazon and the miracle nipples you can order form the Fox Valley website online. Your serval should be put on a raw diet that consists of whole prey. Below is a homemade recipe that can be used as a replacement for whole raw prey from time to time. But keep in mind the best diet you can offer you serval is baby chicks, quail, mice and small rabbits. A variety will make them happy. Also feed a good quality wet canned food 3 times a week. Keep a good quality dry food around for crunching. This helps them keep their teeth clean and strong.

RECIPE:
TWO CHICKEN THIGHS
THREE CHICKEN BREASTS
15 CHICKEN HEARTS
2 WHOLE CHICKEN LIVERS
15 GIZZARDS
4 CHICKEN NECKS
1 HEAPING TABLESPOON OF WHOLE CANNED PUMPKIN
1 TABLESPOON OF WILDTRAX SUPPLEMENT

Grind all the ingredients in the recipe and mix them together. I use the **Gander Mountain #12 Stainless Steel Electric Meat Grinder** Item # 754159. This grinder will come with 3 blades. I start with the blade with the largest holes and grind everything up and mix it together and then I repeat with the 2nd largest blade. This will make about 2 weeks of food. I separate into sandwich sized plastic snap containers and freeze them. I take one out a day to thaw.

Feed them twice a day starting with about 1/2 cup of meat that is warmed for about 45 seconds din the microwave. You can pour about 2 oz. of warmed Fox Valley formula over the top if you want too. Mix it up with a fork and serve.

Make sure it is not too hot. You don't want to burn your baby's mouth. If you do that you are going to have a problem getting them to eat again.

You may need to put your kitten in a small room to eat where he will not be distracted while eating. Most kittens would rather play then eat.

I also feed 10 to 12 pinkie mice every other day. You can graduate to the chicks when they reach about 4 or 5 months. Monitor their fluids and make sure they know where the water is. You may have to pick your kitten up several times throughout the day and carry them to the bowl to remind them to drink water. Water fountains work well. I prefer the ceramic type. Make sure you clean your water bowls and fountains once a week and don't leave the meat mix out for longer than 2 hours. Throw it away or feed it to your adult dogs and cats. Also monitor their poops and make sure they are pooping at least once every 48 hours. If they aren't they could be dehydrated. Make sure they are drinking plenty of fluids. Also you can add some extra whole canned pumpkin to their food.

The Diet will Change as your fur baby matures and they will enjoy a little variety. You can start feeding whole raw chicken legs when they get to be about 4 months old. They will love gnawing on them and it helps keep their teeth strong. I would feed a couple of chicken legs a week. Also a few other things that could be added to the daily diet are raw tilapia, raw shrimp, red meat, 2-3 day old chicks or quail etc. I order my pinkies, quail and chicks from rodentpro.com

Please read this article on Metabolic Bone Disease in Exotic Pets .
http://www.exoticpetvet.net/dvms/mbd2.html.

In the wild the Serval cat is mostly a nocturnal animal but sometimes can be diurnal. Serval Cats are very adaptable and are mainly a terrestrial cat, but can also climb and swim. They hunt in lightly bushed countryside's, grasslands, forests and around marshy places and rivers. Servals primarily hunt alone and are not known to hunt larger prey than themselves. In the tall grass a Serval pounces up and down in pursuit of mice and other rodents. They also probe small holes with their long forepaws in search of prey. Their large ears are very sensitive and can listen to the motion of a rodent as far as 20 feet away. A diet for Servals can vary widely depending on habitat and availability.

A wild servals diet mainly consists of whole meats. So a whole pray diet including innards, fur, and bones is obviously the best diet you could feed your serval. Try to find a supplier of feeder rats, or chicks over 3 days old. You can order from www.rodentpro.com.
A raw diet with added supplements is the second best diet you could provide for your serval. You should feed your serval raw meat with bones, innards and skin included. In the wild, servals eat 80% rodents (mice, rats, rabbits), 14% shrews, and 5% birds, 1% reptiles (frogs and lizards). Domestic servals can be fed assorted grasses, whole raw chicken, whole raw turkey parts, raw beef, raw venison, raw rabbit, raw squirrel, quail, raw fresh fish, and shrimp

It is hazardous to feed cooked meat or poultry with bones to your serval because the bones become very brittle and can splinter. Also make sure any frozen meat is completely thawed because the bones become brittle when frozen. Do not thaw meat in the microwave.

Servals love fresh water fish such as tilapia and will eat chicken hearts like popcorn which is a good natural taurine source. If you decide to feed chicken legs or thighs only, make sure to add a high quality supplement such as oasis, Mazuri, or wild trax to make up for the organs and other parts. Discuss a diet with an exotic cat dietician to get the exact supplement amount needed. Make sure your supplements contain taurine, if you don't feed chicken hearts. Probiotics (plain yogurt) and lysine are other supplements to consider. I usually grind all of my meat parts up and add the supplements if needed. But be careful not to add to many supplements. You have to take into consideration what you are feeding raw and add to that. For example: If you feed 6 chicken hearts a day you don't need to add taurine and if you are feeding bone and chicken necks you don't need to add calcium or phosphorus

Make sure your feeding enough calcium at least 54 mgs of calcium per animal while kittens, tapering off to about 45 – 49 mgs per pound for an adult of three years. Calcium can come from a variety of sources, one being the bones of animals. If your serval isn't offered a raw diet or it doesn't eat large quantities of bone, then supplementing their diet with calcium is a must. Make sure your serval is exposed to direct sunlight daily to insure the proper breakdown of calcium.

When feeding your domestic serval, make sure the food is fresh, cleaned and thoroughly washed before feeding. Servals eat between one and six pounds of meat a day. The amount to feed a healthy adult serval would be 3% of his body weight. For example a 30 pound should eat at least 0.9 pounds of meat a day. For a growing kitten it can be as much as 5% of his body weight. The 3% pertains to real meat weight. Commercial diets like Blue Buffalo and Mazuri are condensed/concentrated and therefore fed in lesser amounts.

The bottom line is that there are a lot of good diets and vitamins out there, but you need to choose what works for your lifestyle and what makes your serval happiest. If your serval is not happy with one diet, he will not thrive as well as being on a diet he enjoys. Let him try some different balanced diets and see what he enjoys the most. You also have to consider what you can afford to feed long term.

Servals are exotic cats with a near domestic dog personality. In a home, they are interesting pets, although large. They get up to 40 pounds. They can jump on your highest appliance, and use it as a perch to watch the goings on in your household. They are very curious and you must cat proof your house if you are going to have one. They love to pounce on anyone's toes and other things that may wiggle under the covers at night. They are most active in the evenings and mornings. They tend to be a one or two person animal, favoring whoever has given them the most attention when they were being raised. You can train them to be more accepting of strangers if you allow them to be around a lot of people while they are growing up. I keep lots of toys around and whenever a new person enters the house I always have them play with the servals first thing. Start this while the servals are very young and they will become a lot more social.

Most places require a permit for exotic pets. Each local is different in their requirements. Some states require permits to breed, other states require them just to have them as pets, and some have no requirements at all. Certain places make it easy as a phone call and visit by the USDA to inspect your facilities. Others have very stringent requirements, often mandating hours of training. At any rate, you must have a secure place for the animals to live, whether it be inside you home, or out in a large spaces enclosure or exhibit.

Serval Kitten Care

Be sure to get a serval kitten at a young age, because they usually bond with their human by the time they are 14 weeks old. I recommend 8 or 9 weeks old. All serval kittens have different personalities. Some are more social than others. But I will list a few important tricks and steps to help you ensure that your new serval kitten will adjust in his or her new home as smoothly as possible. The first thing you do when you get your serval kitten is take the kitten in its carrier to your bedroom away from everyone and let them have some time to adjust to the new smells and sounds around them. Place a litter box in every corner of your room. Place food and water by the entrance of their carrier. Take a worn shirt with your scent on it and place it near the entrance. Open the carrier door and leave the room. Stay away for a hour or two. When you return enter the room very quietly with a string toy in hand. Just sit a distance from the carrier and play with the stick toy to try and get the kittens attention. After about 30 minutes of doing this your kitten should be playing. Start making small attempts to pet the kitten. Do not move to fast and speak in a soft voice. Continue this series of steps for several days until the kitten is comfortable with you. After this you can start to bring one more member of the family in with you one at a time. The trick is to move slow and be patient. After the kitten has proven to be comfortable with you and your bedrooms surroundings then allow him or her to explore the rest of the house. Play with your kitten at least two times a day for at least 30 minutes. Play with the stick toys, teach him to fetch, play tag, tug of war or keep away. Be creative.

Be sure to continually expose your serval kitten to new people and new surroundings. When you have visitors, your serval kitten may run hide and not come out until after the visitors have left. Do not try to force your kitten out in the open for display. If the kitten does come out while visitors are around ask the visitors to play with the kitten. Tell them to speak softly and not to grab at the kitten. This will help the kitten get used to new people and will teach them to enjoy their new friends. Don't be surprised if your serval kitten starts running to get his toys to meet a complete stranger at the door when they arrive. When you find your serval kitten doing something very wrong, it is best to reprimand them with a firm "No" in a deep voice. Body language, and the sound of your voice will become familiar to your kitten and they will learn that this means you're not happy. Servals are very smart and also very stubborn, so it may take several repetitions in order for them to learn that you are not going to let them have their way. Just remember, don't hit your Serval, as they may become scared of you. Timeouts in a kennel or small room is also a good way to correct bad behavior. But remember don't punish bad behavior unless it is seriously wrong like biting or doing something that might endanger you or someone else. But always remember to award good behavior.

Hand raising exotic kittens

When you intend to hand raise exotic cats, 14-17 days is a good time to take on this responsibility. Those first two weeks should be with their mothers because this is the most critical and most serval mothers will do a better job than you can. Just make sure to handle the kittens for at least 15 minutes every day starting at about 5 days. When your serval mother consistently loses litter, remove the kittens at birth. It's tough to make those decisions because you can never be certain. If the kittens are not in immediate danger of dying, allow them at least 48 hours to nurse their mothers so that they will receive her colostrum. Kittens pulled at 2 weeks develop to be just as mellow and docile as those removed earlier. The time for imprinting is when their eyes first open or just before they have the ability to focus up until the time they are 12 weeks old. After they are 12 weeks the time for imprinting is decreasing.

Remember that when you remove the kittens or the litter die's it will cause the mother to go back into heat. You are putting a lot of unnecessary stress on her health and future litters if you allow her to become pregnant again so soon. Keep her separated from the male for at least 8-12 weeks.

Serval kittens haven't had time to develop their own immunity against infections and they rely on immunity in the form of antibodies, passed down from their mothers. Some of these antibodies pass into the kittens while they are still in the womb. The amount of immunity passed to the kittens before birth depends on the health and nutritional status of the mother as well as her vaccination status. But many antibodies are passed along to the kittens in the first milk or colostrum that the mother produces in the first day or two after giving birth. The amount of antibody that can pass through the kittens' intestine in this way begins to decline shortly after birth. After a day or two has passed, the antibodies in milk can no longer be absorbed by the kittens. But the antibody that they did absorb persists in their blood and protects them for many weeks. Kittens that do not receive colostrum are more prone to bacterial infections. It is not until they are about 8 weeks old that kittens are able to produce enough antibodies of their own to protect themselves.

All formula products were originally designed to feed domestic kittens and puppies. Servals produce milk that is richer in fat and protein. Domestic cats have adapted to absorbing sugar by producing a considerable amount of lactase enzyme in their intestines. This capability is not as well developed in servals. That is why they are prone to develop bloating, diarrhea and other digestive problems if they consume products formulated for domestic cats or formulas high in cow's milk.

The most commonly used commercial milk formulas to bottle-feed baby servals are KMR, Milk Matrix 33/40 and Fox valley for kittens. Some people prepare their own formulas from scratch. There are hundreds of formula recipes. You can ask on the very informative Facebook group "The Serval Cat lover". In this group you can communicate with hundreds of serval parents all over the world. When one person prefers one formula over another, it is usually because they think they see less diarrhea and bloat with one or the other product. When problems occur, it appears to be due to the fat portion of the formulas. The differences between product batches and limited product shelf life probably account for the rest of the differences you will see. When the powder is opened it will need to be refrigerated. If the powdered formula you purchase is old or if a particular batch is not up to quality, or if the liquid you prepare was not blended sufficiently or was blended too vigorously, the fat can form clumps that are too large for infants to absorb. PetAg put out an advisory a while ago that electric blenders might cause the fat portion of their products to clump and congeal. When this occurs, the kittens can die from intestinal blockages. So make sure you strain your milk after mixing. Be sure there are no clumps or graininess in the formulas you prepare and that the powder itself shows no sign of off-odor or rancidity. To be used successfully, all dry formulas needs to be well mixed with pre-warmed water. I recommend the formulas only be mixed with warmed water in a container with a whisk ball to remove all clumps. Use a container with a water tight seal. This way you can shake it vigorously with the whisk ball inside. After mixing you can store the container in the refrigerator and continue to mix every time you take it out of the refrigerator

Serval kittens do best when their first few feedings are warmed electrolyte solutions such as half-strength pedialyte. Keep the day's stock supply on the top shelf in your fridge, heating only what you are about to use. Reheating destroys nutrients and changes the consistency of the fat portion. Give the formula time for the air bubbles and foam to leave the bottles. Over the first day or two, gradually change from a pure electrolyte formula to formula composed of three parts electrolyte/water and one part powdered formula. Over the next few days, increase the concentration to two parts water/electrolytes mixed with one part powdered formula. Always begin with a diluted formula until the kitten adjusts to it. Too rich a formula, given too soon can cause something called osmotic diarrhea in which unabsorbed nutrients pull water out of the body and into the intestine. It takes time for kittens to adjust from their mother's nipple to a rubber one. You can place a drop of milk on the cub's tongue and dampen the nipple with the same mixture to help it get the idea. Have patience and just keep trying. Serval kittens do well on 2 oz. kitten nursing bottles but sometimes you have to start with a syringe. A petag nursing nipple or miracle nipple will fit perfectly over the end of a15-20 cc Luer-Lok Tipped syringe. Cubs can be choosy about nipples and bottles. If one brand or style doesn't work, try another. Buy many nipples. If you are using the petag nipple cut a small X in the end of the nipple with fingernail scissors. No milk should drip from the nipple when the bottle is full and held upside down. Shaking the bottle should produce a drop or two. If you use the miracle nipple you want have to worry about whether you cut the x to big or little because the miracle nipple comes with a hole already in it.

Use a bottlebrush and dish detergent to clean bottles and nipples between uses. Boil and rinse the items. Do not warm bottles of milk in the microwave. Microwave a container of water, check its temperature with your finger, and place the bottle of formula in that to warm it. Squirt a little of the formula or your wrist. The milk should be pleasantly warm, not scalding. Never squeeze the bottle when feeding. If you must force feed use a syringe with luer-lok and petag nipple or miracle nipple. You can control the flow of the formula better. Rubber nipples do not last forever so throw them away when they begin to flow on their own.

Feeding every two to three hours, dawn to dusk, is sufficient for most 1 to 2 week old kittens. If the kittens were born weak or are not vigorous nurses, you can feed them every hour for the first few days. It is always safer to feed weak kittens smaller amounts at more frequent intervals than risk the chance they will aspirate larger amounts given less frequently.

By the time the kittens are 3 weeks old, they should do fine when fed every four hours and every 5 hours by the time they reach 5 weeks of age. Feed the weanlings their formula 2-3 times a day. Serval kittens need to drink at least 30% of their body weight each day. Most are vigorous eaters and will eat up to half their body weight in one day. Just keep a check on their tummy while your feeding and do not allow it to eat so much that the belly is tight and bloated. A little bloat without the tightness is ok. Make sure to burp your kitten after each bottle feeding to remove any trapped gases. Stay near 30% of their body weight for the youngest kittens. The risks of overfeeding are greater than the risks of moderately underfeeding. Stop when they aren't greedy for the formula and don't re-feed them before their stomachs have time to empty. If they haven't taken the amount you think they should but their stomachs appear full, stop. Overeating can cause intestinal problems and bloat. If the kittens stay restless and hungry between feedings and their growth rate drops off, try increasing the strength of their formula.

Put more formula in the bottle than they will consume so they don't suck air and don't rush them and let them take breaks during their feedings.

Both male and female kittens are born at about the same weight. It can take up to two days for kittens to begin gaining weight. So it is sufficient if they don't gain weight on their first or second day. From then on, their weight gain should be a rapid slope upward.

It is a good idea to add some multivitamins to formulas if you are making the formula from scratch. I prefer to use a liquid human pediatric vitamin. They are sold under many names, both proprietary and generic. The best known brand is Poly-Vi-Sol Vitamin Drops. They all should contain Vitamins A, C, D, and E, thiamine, riboflavin, niacin, pyridoxine, Vitamin B12 and iron.

Once the serval kitten is in your care, integrate it completely into your life. The more time you spend with it, the more you stroke and cuddle it and the more you talk to it, the better. Allow several different trusted people to hold, cuddle and play with the kittens. This will help him/her adjust to strangers easier in the future.

A Serval Sanctuary

Southern Savannah Sanctuary is a Serval sanctuary located in Southern Alabama. It was started as a service to the serval owners that may find themselves in a situation where they are no longer able to care for their servals. The biggest and saddest reason that most servals are taken away from their owner is due to State bans. Bans are put in place by people who have no education or experience with servals. Their reasoning is based on rumors and false information that is given to them by more inexperienced uneducated people. People fear what they do not understand. These cats are usually taken from loving homes, where they are treated like kings and queens. They are ripped from their family's arms and placed into concrete jails where they end up dying from starvation, loneliness and dehydration. My question is why take a beloved pet from a family that has dedicated their lives and love to taking care of it and turn it over to a concrete jail like facility that has no knowledge about the pet care needed. The workers have no love or regard for them. They just throw them in the jail to rot. This is a shame because the bond that a Serval forms with their owner is very intense and the separation is extremely upsetting for them. They can become so upset that they refuse to eat. They can also seem wild again only because they are scared of their strange surroundings. Rehoming is a hard thing and it takes a special person with a lot of Serval knowledge and patients to be able to help the sad, and emotionally upset serval adjust to their new environment. Not only do you have to understand how to supply a well-rounded nutritional diet plan and health care program, but you have to understand how to read their temperament, body language, and vocal sounds. I have had over 20 years' experience with exotic cats and have studied them and researched them endlessly.

None of the Domestic Servals you see today were taken from the wild. Servals have been kept as companions for thousands of years. Pictures of beloved servals have been found on tomb walls from the Egyptian times. The servals roamed freely in and around temples and residences guarding grain stores and even pulling small wagons to haul supplies throughout the villages. The domestic servals behavior and temperament is different than the servals still living in the wild. Some of the blood lines you find throughout the world today have been domesticated for centuries. Every generation of domestic serval leads to a more docile and intelligent cat. Servals have proven over and over again that they can live with and among humans happily and being able to do this will insure their existence. They make unforgettable companions to their pet owners. It does take a special animal person to own one, but once you bond with a serval, they are friends for life.

Over the years I have learned a lot about the characteristics and habits of the serval. Each individual serval is domesticated to a different level. Some know no strangers and will happily play fetch with anyone that is willing and some will only pick 2 or three people to bond with.

A serval can be a lap cat to their owner but when they are taken away from their original owner, they can become very hard to handle. In order to change their behavior you have to spend a lot of time around them. The main thing you have to understand is that you have to earn their trust and this may take months, but just stay patient, calm and non-threatening toward your serval and soon they will start to calm down. Servals are very smart and they have survived on this earth for thousands of years, so the fact that some are very skittish and will run from anything new and suspicious, is really a good thing. So it is important to understand that if you run after and chase a serval they most likely will run away. You will have better success trying to get the serval to come to you. Never raise your voice, hit them, or throw something at them. Let them come to you on their own terms and don't make them do anything against their own will, except in the case of an emergency.

Rehoming Servals

Kaos, a 3 year old male serval, was rehomed three times before he ended up with me. When I first got him, Kaos was scared and depressed. I had to work with him for weeks to win his trust. I am lucky to have any kind of relationship with him. At first I was the only one brave enough to enter the cage with him. I would sit for hours with my laptop or book in his enclosure. It took 9 weeks before he decided he would sit in the chair beside me. One thing I do that he can't resist is to take a nice soft, fluffy blanket into his enclosure and spread it out on the ground and sit down on it. In no time at all, he will come lay down beside me and put his head in my lap. He can be a lap cat when he wants to be but most of the time he just wants to be left alone. Rehoming a serval is a very hard thing to do and I would not recommend it unless the new owner is very experienced and patient with exotic animals. You must fully understand that you may never have a friendly relationship with a rehomed serval. But I have had pretty good luck with my rehomed servals. I recommend starting with a young well socialized, human imprinted serval around 9 weeks old.

Since Kaos, I have acquired 6 more servals. Tiki was 2 years old and about as hard as Kaos to bond with. Shera was a one year old serval and took to me almost immediately. Shera is a very sweet and loving serval and is one of the most affectionate servals I have ever encountered. Ziva was a 4 week old serval kitten when I got her. She came from a breeder who was having trouble getting her to eat. Ziva's breeder took her to the vet several times for treatments and tests but still she would not eat. When I got her I took her to Andrews Avenue animal Hospital in Ozark Alabama and they kept her for several days running tests and lab work and finally found out that she had a very bad kidney infection. The Vet kept her for a few days longer and she surprisingly got better. When she came home we still had to hand feed her. In took a few weeks more but she started to regain her strength and was able to eat on her on. Ziva developed a very strong bond with my husband because on the days I had to work he would sneak her into work, and put her in a box under his desk in order to be able to hand feed her every two hours.

My other servals are Puma, Mojo and Zandy. Puma and mojo were born at the sanctuary and Zandy is retired from a traveling zoo. I love them all and have committed my life to them. It's not bad being a serval servant.

Puma

mojo

Zandy and zeva

tiki

Kaos

kka

kaos

Kaos

Zeva and Kaos

shera

Mojo

Serval Kitten

Shera

puma

Me and Shera

Mojo

Shera watching me work on the water fall

Zandy loves water

shera